Rookie
biographies™

Thomas Jefferson

By Simone T. Ribke

Consultant
Jeanne Clidas, Ph.D.
National Reading Consultant
and
Professor of Reading, SUNY Brockport

Children's Press®
A Division of Scholastic Inc.
New York   Toronto   London   Auckland   Sydney
Mexico City   New Delhi   Hong Kong
Danbury, Connecticut

Designer: Herman Adler Design
Photo Researcher: Caroline Anderson
The photo on the cover shows Thomas Jefferson.

Library of Congress Cataloging-in-Publication Data

Ribke, Simone T.
  Thomas Jefferson / by Simone T. Ribke ; consultant, Jeanne Clidas.
      p. cm. – (Rookie biographies)
Includes index.
  ISBN 0-516-25884-2 (lib. bdg.)   0-516-27927-0 (pbk.)
  1. Jefferson, Thomas, 1743-1826–Juvenile literature. 2.
Presidents–United States–Biography–Juvenile literature. [1.
Jefferson, Thomas, 1743-1826. 2. Presidents.] I. Clidas, Jeanne. II.
Title. III. Series. IV. Series: Rookie biography.
  E332.79.R53 2003
  973.4'6'092–dc21

                              2003004513

CHILDREN'S PRESS, and ROOKIE BIOGRAPHIES™, and associated
logos are trademarks and or registered trademarks of Scholastic Library
Publishing. SCHOLASTIC and associated logos are trademarks and or
registered trademarks of Scholastic Inc.
13 14 15 16 17   15 14 13 12

Thomas Jefferson was the third president of the United States.

He was born on April 13, 1743, in Virginia. At that time, America was made up of 13 colonies (KOL-uh-neez). Virginia was one of them.

Colonies are made up of people who leave their homes to move to a new place.

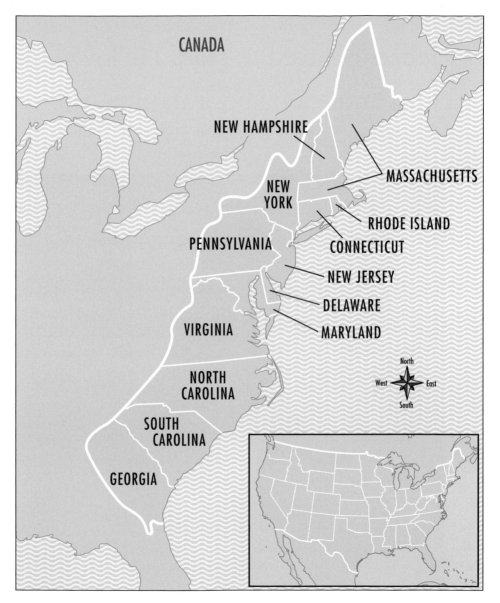

CANADA

NEW HAMPSHIRE

MASSACHUSETTS

NEW YORK

RHODE ISLAND

CONNECTICUT

PENNSYLVANIA

NEW JERSEY

DELAWARE

MARYLAND

VIRGINIA

North

West East

South

NORTH CAROLINA

SOUTH CAROLINA

GEORGIA

5

Jefferson loved to read. He loved to hike and learn about nature, too.

He also played the violin.

Jefferson went to college when he was 16. He worked hard and became a lawyer.

A lawyer is a person who helps people understand the law.

In 1768, Jefferson made
plans to build a big house.

He called his home Monticello
(mahn-teh-SEH-loh). Jefferson
and his wife, Martha, moved in.

At this time, the 13 colonies were ruled by Britain. Many people felt that the British laws and taxes were unfair.

The colonists went to war against Britain in 1775. They wanted to be a free country.

Jefferson wrote the Declaration of Independence (dek-luh-RAY-shuhn of in-di-PEN-duhnss). This important paper told why the colonies did not want to be ruled by Britain.

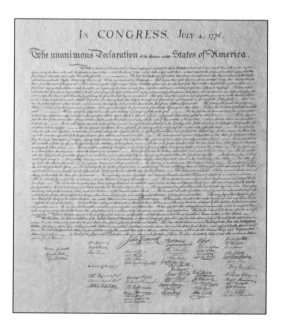

Jefferson wrote the main part.
Then other people added
their ideas.

When the war was over, the colonies were free from British laws. The colonies formed a new country called the United States of America.

George Washington became the first president.

17

John Adams

After Washington retired in 1797, the country voted for its next president.

Jefferson ran against his friend John Adams. Adams won by three votes.

Four years later, Jefferson ran for president again. This time he won.

Jefferson was the second president to live in the White House.

Jefferson did many important
things. He bought land from
the French. It was called the
Louisiana Territory.

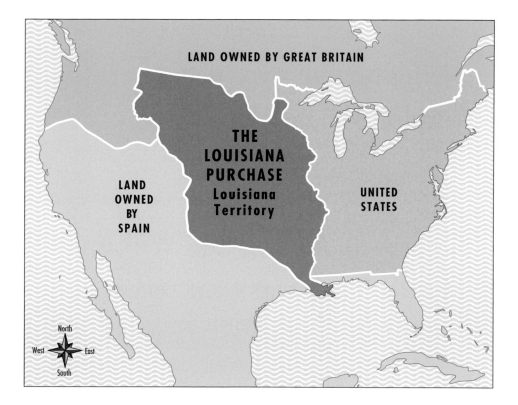

Jefferson sent two men to explore the new land.

The men's names were Meriwether Lewis and William Clark. Their trip went very well.

Jefferson was elected president again in 1804. After he finished his second term, he retired to his home in Monticello.

He liked to invent things. His inventions made it easier to do jobs like plowing.

Thomas Jefferson died on
July 4, 1826.

Jefferson did many great things
in his life. He helped shape the
United States.

Words You Know

colonies

Declaration of Independence

George Washington

inventions

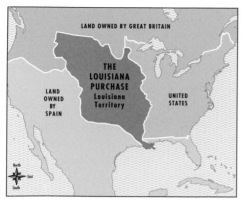

Louisiana Territory

Monticello

Thomas Jefferson

White House

Index

About the Author

Simone T. Ribke grew up on a horse farm in Maryland and now lives in New York City. She has a degree in education and writes children's books. Simone loves playing football and spending time with her cat.

Photo Credits

Photographs © 2003: Bridgeman Art Library International Ltd., London/New York/Brooklyn Museum of Art, New York, USA: 17, 30 bottom left; Corbis Images/Bettmann: 20, 22; Folio, Inc.: 6 (Everett C. Johnson), 26 (Fred J. Maroon); Hulton|Archive/Getty Images: 21, 31 bottom right; Monticello/Thomas Jefferson Foundation, Inc.: 27, 30 bottom right; Photo Researchers, NY: 7 (Grantpix), 18 (Tom McHugh/National Portrait Gallery, Wash., DC); Photri Inc.: cover, 3, 10, 13, 31 top right, 31 bottom left; Stock Montage, Inc.: 15; Superstock, Inc.: 25 (David David Gallery), 14, 29, 30 top right; The Image Works: 5; Unicorn Stock Photos/Andre Jenny: 9.

Maps by Bob Italiano